BY THE GRACE OF G-D

ADVICE
FOR LIFE

DAILY LIFE

Adapted freely from the teachings of
The Rebbe
Rabbi Menachem Mendel Schneerson
of righteous memory

Compiled and adapted by
Dovid Zaklikowski

Photos by
Marc Asnin, Michel Setboun
& Joe Chahwan

HASIDIC
archives

Advice for Life: Daily Life © Hasidic Archives

First edition 2015
Second edition 2016

www.HasidicArchives.com
HasidicArchives@gmail.com
Facebook.com/HasidicArchives

. . . .

. . . .

ISBN 978-1-944875-01-5

Design by Design is Yummy and Hasidic Archives Studios

Printed in Malaysia

For the memory of
Lorne Rozovsky

Contents

INTRODUCTION • 7

DAILY GRIND • 11

HEALTH • 43

BUSINESS • 61

HOME • 73

INTERPERSONAL • 81

PURPOSE • 103

ESSAYS ON LIFE • 131

GLOSSARY • 148

SOURCES AND CREDITS • 150

ACKNOWLEDGEMENTS • 153

The Rebbe, Rabbi Menachem Mendel Schneerson

Introduction

The Rebbe, Rabbi Menachem Mendel Schneerson, of righteous memory, is recognized as one of the most brilliant minds of the last century. He authored numerous scholarly volumes, and is distinguished for his remarkable commentaries on the Talmud, Maimonides' magnum opus on Jewish law, and the classic biblical commentator Rabbi Shlomo Yitzchaki (Rashi).

He is remembered for his correspondences with myriads of Jews and non-Jews. Piles of letters arrived on his desk daily; he studied each, personally responding to most. His letters were as reassuring as they were instructional. The Rebbe would often, in a mere line or two, reach to the heart of the matter and direct the individual on a sure path.

Central to the Rebbe's approach was that every person could and should make his or her own decision. The Rebbe would encourage people to recognize their own capabilities. Regarding medical issues, he would direct the person to a specialist in that field. To rabbinical queries, the Rebbe would instruct people to contact a local rabbi or rabbinical expert.

Rabbi Dr. Tzvi Hersh Weinreb, a psychologist and currently the executive vice president emeritus of the OU, stated, "I personally benefited from the Rebbe's advice in a life-changing telephone conversation I had with him more than forty years ago. Thousands of others have benefited similarly."

Rabbi Dr. Weinreb summarized various ideas that were frequently found in the Rebbe's correspondence:

- It is important to have clear and achievable goals in life.

- When those goals are reached, you need to set new goals and never be complacent.

- Study, joy and a focus on helping others are antidotes to depression.

- Cultivate as many friendships as possible, by giving spiritually or materially to another person.

- Persist in the face of failure. Failure is seldom total and never final; it is usually a step toward reaching the next level of achievement.

- Never compromise religious principles; such compromise is ineffective.

- You have a distinct role to play; G-d and your fellow rely on you to accomplish it. No one else can do what you are uniquely created to do.

This current selection of advice, the eighth in our ongoing series entitled "Advice for Life," is compiled from many sources, mainly from the Rebbe's correspondence. The material is adapted from the original sources, and any errors are my own. In addition, I included several stories based on firsthand accounts.

It is my hope that you find meaning in this collection and share it with others.

Dovid Zaklikowski

DAILY GRIND

Success

Our world is never complete.
Therefore, although we strive
for the best outcomes,
we should also accept and
celebrate partial success
in our endeavors.

Bliss?

Life is not a blissful experience; we constantly need to seek inspiration from those around us in order to cope with challenges. When it comes to spiritual matters, we should look to those who have achieved greater status than ourselves. When it comes to material matters, we should seek out the less fortunate so that we can appreciate the relativity of life, and all that G-d has given us.

Keeping Occupied

One should always be occupied. The lack of occupation can cause one to focus and overly obsess on the minute details of life, which in turn can lead to depression and mood swings. Busying oneself with a job, volunteering, learning, or influencing others is the antidote.

Purpose

When looking for purpose
in your day-to-day life,
leave the comfort
of your surroundings
—at least twice a week—
to help others in need.

Choice

In contrast to G-d's other
creations, humans were created
with free will. We can choose
either to be destructive or to
perform good deeds, thereby
uplifting ourselves and everyone
around us. G-d gave us Judaism
to guide us to the correct path.

Return

Nothing goes to waste, not your thoughts, speech or actions. What you did yesterday stays with you today. It may seem like your past deeds are gone, but G-d has given you the unique ability to master your past and change it for the better. All you have to do is regret the past and pledge to follow the just and righteous path going forward.

Evil's Limits

Do not dwell on your strengths or your
shortcomings. Thinking about the negative will
weaken your will to improve. The good you do is
connected to G-dliness and is infinite. The bad
you have done is intrinsically limited and will be
erased when you return to G-d's ways.

The Atom in You

Do you feel insignificant and unable to make a difference in the world? The tiny atom demonstrates that strength is more important than size. Even your smallest actions may have enormous ramifications, affecting you, those around you and the entire universe.

G-d's Love

G-d says, "I love you" (Malachi 1:2). Nothing you do can change that.

G-d's Envoy

What is joy? Contemplating
how G-d chose you to be His
personal envoy in this world
inspires humility and joy.

The Power of One

We could easily believe that one person cannot effect global change. But we have seen, in the twentieth century, an individual who almost destroyed the civilized world. If he could change the world with evil, surely we can do it with holiness and goodness.

Many Creatures, One Human

During the six days of creation, every creature was given a mate. Only man was created alone. This emphasizes that we, alone, have the power to bring the entire world to perfection.

IT'S NOT ALL ABOUT YOU

Marc Wilson was facing a dark period in his life after the collapse of his second marriage and the disintegration of his rabbinical career. Shortly after, he headed to New York, where he met the Rebbe and discussed his plans to devote more time to writing.

The Rebbe advised, "Sometimes a devoted layperson can do incalculably more good than a rabbi."

The Rebbe added, "They say that you were once a student of Rabbi Aaron Soloveitchik. I am making a gift to charity in the hope that you make peace with him." Rabbi Soloveitchik had been Marc's teacher at the Hebrew Theological College in Chicago, Illinois, and the two had a rocky relationship.

For Marc, the Rebbe's words had a deep impact.

Over the years, Marc's depression deepened, and eventually he was spending most of his day watching television from bed. Life, he felt, left him no options. He would pen articles about his dark life. Marc surmised, "There are plenty of depressed people who like reading stories about depressed people."

On his next visit to Crown Heights, the Rebbe instructed Marc, "You should teach."

"The Rebbe obviously understood," said Marc, "that to heal from depression, I needed to start giving to others."

However, the following year likewise passed in a depressive blur in which Marc did not heed the Rebbe's counsel. Again he found himself at the Rebbe's door.

The Rebbe then suggested: "You should teach. Anything, perhaps Talmud, even if it is only to one or two people in your living room."

Soon afterwards Marc began to lead a class in Talmud, and his life was altered forever.

The Rebbe (right) with Israeli President Zalman Shazar, 1971.

Self-Respect

To succeed, you must have self-respect. If you do not respect yourself, it is unlikely that others will respect you. When you give up on a task, the message you project to others who may have wanted to partner with you in the future is that you are incompetent.

" " Your Virtues

We need to recognize the virtues, strengths and talents that G-d has given us, without succumbing to haughtiness. We must recognize, as our sages say, that every person is an entire world.

The Effort

All matters of goodness
are born of great effort,
courage and fortitude.
In fact, when you
obtain something through
effort and toil,
it is far more valuable and
brings you
greater satisfaction.

Moving On

When looking to move
ahead in life,
seek a situation
in which benefits
are greater and
deficits are fewer.
Perfection is nonexistent.
If you cannot find it,
or it seems as though
the situation won't
change significantly,
stay where you are
and make the best of it.

Speech

When in doubt, relay the issue to an individual with whom you can speak openly and honestly. Very often, simply articulating the problem to another engenders clarity.

" " Thoughts

Do not wage war with your bad and worrisome
thoughts and feelings; just remove your mind
from them. Removing your mind from them is
accomplished by replacing the negative thoughts
with unrelated positive ones. Even better is to
replace them with words of prayer
and Jewish teachings.

The Flame

You need to take the initiative in inspiring others to do good. You can never know how vast your impact might be, since it begins with kindling just one flame. That spark can, in turn, light many more.

Your Capabilities

Generally, a person—a boss, perhaps—
won't assign you a responsibility that is
beyond your ability. Similarly, G-d will
not burden you with tasks that are not in
your capacity to perform.

Uplifting

When you set aside part of your income
for the purpose of charity, you are not
"losing" money. Rather, you uplift
the money, and yourself,
to even greater heights.

WHEN THINGS ARE IN TURMOIL

The young, quiet Bostonian, Rabbi Yehuda Krinsky, kept to himself through the duration of his studies at the Lubavitch Yeshivah. He was the son of immigrants who created a large, thriving and observant home during a time when Jewish practice was in decline in the United States.

A short while before Rabbi Krinsky's marriage, the Rebbe's assistant, Rabbi Chaim Mordechai Aizik Hodakov, asked him what he planned to do for a living. The young man responded that he still had no concrete plans. Rabbi Hodakov then asked the 23-year-old groom if he wanted to join the Rebbe's secretariat. Rabbi Krinsky was astonished at the request and enthusiastically responded in the affirmative.

During his first week of employment, the Rebbe called Rabbi Krinsky into his office. When he entered, he found the Rebbe correcting a letter draft. The Rebbe had made numerous corrections and asked Rabbi Krinsky to retype the letter. The task was daunting; the letter was replete with changes between and atop the lines, with arrows in every direction pointing to further changes.

The Rebbe guided Rabbi Krinsky how to decipher the letter: "Start from the beginning. Retype it word after word, line after line. In the end, you will see that everything works out okay."

The young aide took this lesson to heart as a life lesson for finding clarity when things look confusing and disjointed.

The Rebbe writing in his study, 1966.

Spiritual Heights

At birth your soul descends from the spiritual

heights of heaven to the lowly physical world.

It is your duty to elevate the physical world to a

spiritual plane by performing good

deeds and kindness.

Quantity or Quality

Look at the six days of creation. Most of the days were used for the creation of the sky, earth, vegetation and living creatures. Yet the single purpose of creation was humanity. In our lives too, most of the day we sleep, eat and work hard to survive; only a small part of our time is dedicated to spiritual pursuits. G-d wants us to know that it is not the quantity of time we spend on spiritual matters that counts; it is the quality of the time that is important.

HEALTH

The Doctor

G-d gives the doctor permission
—and, by extension, the ability—
to heal. Thus, it is incumbent
upon us to listen to a doctor's
instructions. This is all the more
relevant when we recognize that
the human body is the property
of G-d, and we are merely its
safe-keeper.

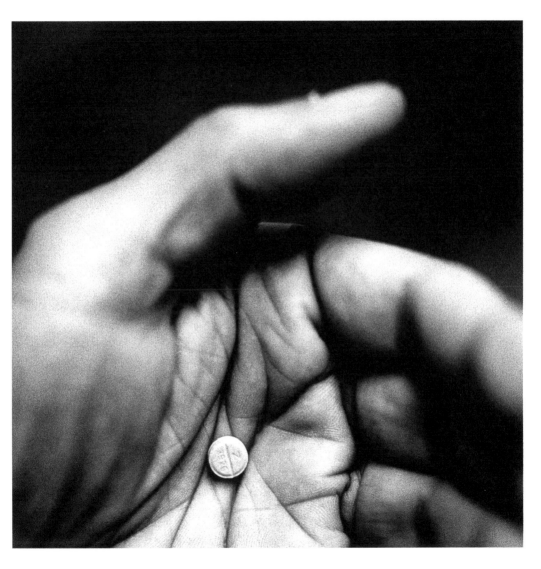

THE FEELINGS OF THE ELDERLY

Before arriving in Israel in 1961, Berke Chein ran a family business on the Russian black market. The family entered this field because it permitted them to live under the Communist regime without having to work on Shabbat. Berke managed the finances, and developed professional aptitude and skill in his department.

Upon his arrival in Israel, he was tasked with managing funds collected from the Chabad community in Israel and earmarked for Chabad in New York. Berke, with his long white beard and penetrating eyes, became iconic in the Chabad community in Israel.

Donations were collected by delegates in Chabad communities across Israel, and then forwarded to Berke, who would organize the funds. Rabbi Ephraim Wolff, director of Chabad in Israel, would then send the money to New York.

While the Chabad community grew in size, Berke aged. In 1988, several Chabad officials considered hiring another person to assist him.

Rabbi Ephraim Wolff asked the Rebbe if he should discuss the idea with Berke.

The Rebbe responded (paraphrased): "If he is advised that he needs assistance, he might believe that he is thought of as weak and without strength to complete his job. This will hurt his feelings. Thus, it is best to continue the collection the way it is, even if the circumstances are not ideal."

The Rebbe in conversation while distributing dollars for charity, 1992.

Dieting

When dieting, we need to ask ourselves essential questions regarding "why" we are eating, and less so about "what" we are eating. Are you eating because you are hungry or craving a certain food, or are you eating to be healthy and productive?

If we obsess over dieting, the entire day revolves around food. This creates constant cravings and frustration, which may cause you to eat even more.

Additionally, a drastic change in eating habits can ultimately cause your weight to boomerang. Gradual changes have a longer-lasting effect.

Strengthen your inner self and serve G-d joyously. This will make your day brighter, boost your metabolism, and assist you in losing weight.

PROTECTING THE VULNERABLE

As the procession of the casket of Rabbi Shlomo Horenstein, a relative of the Rebbe and a respected rabbinical figure, passed Lubavitch world headquarters, the Rebbe inquired about his elderly widow's wellbeing. He was told she was feeling sickly. The Rebbe instructed her that she need not continue on to the cemetery.

Yet when Mrs. Horenstein still wanted to go, the Rebbe advised that she ask a rabbi. Rabbi Dovber Rivkin listened to the quandary, and responded that Mrs. Horenstein need not go to the burial. She, however, insisted that she wanted to go.

The Rebbe responded, "A rabbi just ruled according to Jewish law that you should not go." Still resilient, she continued to protest, so the Rebbe said to her, "Perhaps you should travel only to the edge of the city, and then return home."

The Rebbe followed the hearse partially by foot and then by car to the Manhattan home of Rabbi Mordechai Shlomo Friedman, leader of the Boyaner hasidic dynasty, of whom Rabbi Horenstein had been a follower. There the Rebbe exited the car and waited for Rabbi Friedman to descend the stairs.

Rabbi Friedman was frail, and walked down the stairs slowly. There was a large crowd of mourners in attendance, and the Rebbe feared for the elderly leader's safety. The Rebbe asked Rabbi Friedman's aides if it is respectful in their circles to assist the elderly rabbi, and they responded in the affirmative. The Rebbe placed his hand under Rabbi's Friedman's arm and protected him from the crowd.

The two esteemed figures spoke briefly, and when they had walked some six feet, the Rebbe told the elderly rabbi that they had accompanied the hearse for the appropriate distance. They returned to Rabbi Friedman's home, where the Rebbe wished him a sweet new year, and waited until Rabbi Friedman was safely inside before departing.

The Rebbe (right) walks beside Rabbi Mordechai Shlomo Friedman while attending a funeral.

Depressing Dreams

Dreams emerge naturally from the contents of our thoughts during the day. Seeking to interpret your dreams, being bothered by negative matter, or fearing dark forebodings comes from the evil inclination. When one overcomes the inclination to become despondent over details of a dream, the good inclination is victorious.

A HOSPITAL IS FOR HEALING

During the Holocaust, Rabbi Yekusiel Yehudah Halberstam was wounded by a stray bullet. He didn't want to go to the clinic in the Nazi concentration camp, for fear of his life. Instead, he plucked a leaf from a tree and covered his wound. Three days later his wound healed, and he made a resolution that if he survived the war, he would build a hospital.

His criterion for his dream institution was that "the doctors and nurses would believe that there is a G-d in this world. They would know that when they attend to the sickly, they are fulfilling one of the greatest commandments of Judaism."

Rabbi Halberstam later became the leader of the Sanz-Klausenberg hasidic dynasty. He kept his word, and in 1976 he initiated the building of the medical center Laniado Home for the Sick. The hospital was named after the brothers Alphonse and Yaakov Avraham Laniado, who donated a vast sum to the cause.

Seeking a blessing and a letter of approbation for the new hospital, Rabbi Halberstam sent a delegation to the Rebbe. There Rabbi Binyomin Wulliger, a diamond dealer and a confidant of Rabbi Halberstam, described the endeavor to the Rebbe. The Rebbe responded, "What is needed is financial assistance. A letter from the Lubavitcher Rebbe will not pay the bills."

The Rebbe then wrote a check with the accompanying instructions: "Make sure to cash the check. If you want to make a copy to show that I support the hospital, you may do so, as long as you make use of these funds."

The hospital was also considering a nursing school, but Rabbi Halberstam was concerned it would attract students who would not adhere to the hospital's religious ethos. The Rebbe responded, "You do not have to worry about who will attend. If the school creates the appropriate atmosphere, this will generate an attitude in the spirit you seek to craft."

The Rebbe then explained that the hospital

Rabbi Halberstam (right) tours the Sanz Center for Health: Laniado Hospital.

should be given a more popular name, such as Sanz. He added that the name of the hospital should have a positive connotation: "A sick person goes to the hospital for a cure. Why call the hospital a Home for the Sick? Call it a Home for Healing."

The hospital's name was changed to "Sanz Center for Health: Laniado Hospital."

The Natural Order

Every individual's health needs to be tended to maximally within the natural order. However, one should place their faith in the Healer of all, for whom the doctor here below acts as a surrogate.

Smoking

Cigarette smoking is not good for your health. As physical health deteriorates, it causes your spiritual health to wane.

Regret

Never regret your pregnancy; accept it as a blessing. One day, when you may want another child, G-d may recall your earlier regrets and heed the message.

ALL THE FACULTIES UNTIL 120!

Rabbi Chaim Yitzchak Poupko, a respected rabbinical figure in Brooklyn, frequently joined the Rebbe's hasidic gatherings at Lubavitch world headquarters. The Rebbe would at times turn to Rabbi Poupko and ask if he had any comment on the scholarly talk.

The rabbi became ill, and was too weak to continue attending the gatherings. Many years later, on the occasion of his grandson's thirteenth birthday, he decided to bring him on a visit to the Rebbe.

Upon seeing Rabbi Poupko, the Rebbe exclaimed, "I haven't seen you for a long time! It's most probable that during this time you have paved innovative approaches in scholarly Jewish learning."

Rabbi Poupko felt that the Rebbe was giving him a blessing, and responded that he hoped it would come to fruition.

The Rebbe responded, "I can only give the blessing, but you have to fulfill it by yourself."

The elderly rabbi realized that the Rebbe was indicating that learning should not diminish even as one ages. Rabbi Poupko wittily responded that though he is an elderly man, he hadn't lost his faculties.

The Rebbe then said, "As it says regarding Moses, he lived until the age of 120, but 'his eyes were not dim, nor his natural force abated' (Deut. 34:6)."

With a smile, the Rebbe added, "You still have a long time until then…"

The Rebbe (right) speaks with Rabbi Chaim Yitzchak Poupko beside Lubavitch world headquarters.

BUSINESS

ANOTHER'S LIVELIHOOD

Mottel Schusterman was a recent immigrant when he began his career in the printing business. He began as a typesetter for the Chabad-Lubavitch publishing house. He often worked with handwritten manuscripts and other texts that needed to be retyped. Over the years, Mr. Schusterman successfully published many volumes of Chabad teachings.

In 1965, Mr. Schusterman received a call from the Rebbe's office. He was told: "It is of immediate importance to begin typesetting the *Hemshech Samech-Vov,*" a series of fundamental hasidic discourses on Chabad philosophy by the fifth Chabad rebbe, Rabbi Shalom Dovber Schneersohn, previously published only in mimeograph form.

Mr. Schusterman immediately went to work that evening. Word spread that publication of the material was imminent, and excitement grew in the Chabad community.

However, a few weeks later he received a call from the Rebbe's office in which he was instructed to immediately stop working on the project. There was no explanation.

Six months later the Rebbe's brother-in-law, Rabbi Shemaryahu Gurary, asked the Rebbe why he had stopped the printing.

The Rebbe responded, "I received a letter from someone who prints the discourse. Much of his livelihood is reliant on that publication, and every penny he earns is important for his survival..."

The Rebbe delivers a scholarly talk, circa 1970.

Disappointment

It is only normal to feel
disappointed when a potential
business partner does not wish
to participate in a venture.
However, when you recognize that
everything is orchestrated by G-d,
it is essentially great news that the
business opportunity never
came to fruition.

Business Focus

Toiling for a living is not just about
making more money. When we
consciously infuse our workday
with the awareness that with our
livelihood we will be able to serve
G-d and make the world a better
place, our daily activities
become holy.

Negative Business

If a business is engaged
in causing harm or
discomfort to others,
why would you want
to take part in
such a venture?

Constant Worry

If a business is unstable,
it is unwise to invest.
Instead of fearing that
you may lose your
investment—though it may
promise a larger profit—
it is advisable to enter
calmer waters.
Though the profit margin
may be lower,
a stable investment
will allow for
more peaceful
living.

A New Occupation

Until there is a
better position
available to you,
don't leave your
current occupation.

Mother on the Job

Mothers can also be involved in the workplace, especially in the field of education. However, the education and upbringing of her children takes priority. Every mother should calculate how much time she should and can work.

Livelihood Attitude

When earning a living, there are two aspects to consider. First, you must make efforts to improve your livelihood through hard work and effort. Second, it is critical to trust that G-d will provide all that you need.

The biblical verse states, "G-d, your G-d, will bless you in all that you do" (Deut. 15:18). This means that your participation and action is required in order to create a vessel for G-d's blessings.

HOME

Protection

When looking from the outside, a home protects from the
frigid weather, the rain and heat. When one is inside, the home
is a cozy place where the individual peacefully resides. A home
also protects us from unwanted influences, those that pour on
us from above and those that want to flood us from below. It
also provides us a sanctuary where we could serenely make
a difference in others lives – where kindness and sunlight
encompasses those who we come in contact with.

Permanent

Purchasing a home is an act that profoundly
ties the purchaser—and all that he wishes to accomplish—
to a specific location. As such, one shouldn't act
hastily in buying a home, but should wait until
one is indeed certain that this is
where he'd like to settle.

Smile Back

What is gained by sustaining fruitless, painful and endless debates with family members? Talk about neutral subjects that do not cause friction. When you are pleasant, our sages say, this provokes a mirror response in the other, which ultimately creates a positive change in the dynamic.

Change

The best way to influence family members toward a better life is by being a good example and leading an upstanding life yourself. However, if immediate change is necessary, the best way to influence them is through their friends.

TREAT CHILDREN EQUALLY

In the aftermath of the Holocaust, Rabbi Hirschel Kotlarsky was the sole survivor of his family. Following a difficult journey which led him through Lithuania, Russia, Japan, China and Canada, he arrived in New York, where he took a position as an assistant to Rabbi Shmaryahu Gurary, the elder son-in-law of the sixth Chabad rebbe. In 1946 he married Goldie Shimelman.

On Sukkot of 1947 his son Yaakov Dovid was born. For the Holocaust survivor with a harrowing history, the birth of a child brought tremendous comfort.

When the child's 13th birthday arrived, Rabbi Kotlarsky was delighted, as it would be the first opportunity for him to make a grand bar mitzvah celebrating Jewish continuity, an obvious response to those who attempted to obliterate the Jewish nation. The Kotlarskys planned to make a large party a week after the birthday, so that they could celebrate in a hall, rather than outside in the *sukkah* hut.

When Rabbi Kotlarsky informed the Rebbe regarding their plans, the Rebbe inquired why they were delaying the celebration. Rabbi Kotlarsky explained that they'd never manage to make a grand celebration on Sukkot, due to limited space in the *sukkah*.

The Rebbe said, "You could make it in the *sukkah*, and if needed, make the *sukkah* larger."

When Rabbi Kotlarsky observed that they wouldn't be able to invite their entire guest list, the Rebbe responded, "So it will be a smaller crowd."

It was clear that the Rebbe believed it was important for the celebration to be observed on the birthday.

The event was celebrated at their home, and while the crowd was small, the event was joyous.

When the 13th birthday of their younger

The Rebbe at a children's gathering, circa early 1960s.

son Moshe arrived, the Rebbe advised Rabbi Kotlarsky based on a Talmudic passage: One should not differentiate between children in a family (Shabbat 10b).

The Rebbe said, "As the celebration for your older son was in your home, the celebration of your younger son should also be at home."

INTERPERSONAL

The Middle

Opinions and thought patterns differ
widely between people. We need to
recognize that this is the way G-d
created humans. The task at hand is to
find a middle ground. This becomes
easier when we recall that we come
from the same father and mother,
Adam and Eve.

The Goal

Feuding parties often forget that
they may have shared a similar goal.
Therefore, the two sides may need to
set their egos aside and allow the joint
goal to take precedence and
provide direction.

DO NOT DIFFERENTIATE BETWEEN OTHERS

Mr. Zalmon Jaffe, a Manchester, England, businessman, would never consider missing the Rebbe's 80th birthday celebration in the spring of 1982. To this monumental event hundreds of dignitaries, philanthropists and community leaders from across the globe would be traveling to partake in the festivities at Lubavitch world headquarters. The Rebbe would deliver scholarly talks, interspersed with intervals of hasidic melodies. Commonly, many of the visitors would deliver gifts to the Rebbe, such as antique scholarly volumes, keys to new institutions and honorary proclamations.

The offices of Lubavitch of Manchester wanted to present the Rebbe with a unique gift accompanied by a birthday greeting. A member of the community purchased a beautiful silver wine decanter, and opined that it would be an ideal gift for the Rebbe. At gatherings, the Rebbe would have a bottle of wine in a plain brown paper bag by his side, and the Manchester community felt that a silver decanter would be appropriate.

Mr. Jaffe was unsure if the Rebbe would use the decanter, and telephoned the Rebbe's wife, with whom he was on close terms. He explained his anxiety regarding the gift, and asked her to inquire of the Rebbe whether he'd appreciate it. The next day Mr. Jaffe called back, and the Rebbetzin informed him that she had given the message to the Rebbe, but the Rebbe had remained silent.

The community decided that the Rebbe's silence confirmed that he would accept the gift. Mr. Jaffe wrote to the Rebbetzin, thanking her for her cooperation and informing her that they planned to present the decanter to the Rebbe on his birthday.

Shortly thereafter, Mr. Jaffe received a letter from

The Rebbe in conversation with Mr. Zalmon Jaffe, 1975.

the Rebbe, with the envelope stamped "Special Delivery, Express." The letter was complete with a blessing, a Jewish teaching and a postscript:

> Mrs. Schneerson has mentioned to me about the question of a silver wine decanter. I certainly appreciate the good intention and desire. But for practical considerations, I must take the thought for the deed. For, as a matter of principle and practice over the past 30-odd years, I prefer to use a "bagged" glass container that conceals its contents, though I have, thank G-d, silver vessels.

> I cannot go into the reasons for the above here. But one reason, if it will satisfy you, is that I do not wish to make a distinction between me and those surrounding me.

Zalmon and Roslyn Jaffe.

DO NOT PUBLICIZE

Shamir is a social and religious organization that assists immigrants from Eastern European countries in acclimating to the job market in Israel. One year, shortly before their annual dinner, the organization's leadership and dinner honorees came to meet with the Rebbe and receive his blessing.

The dinner chairman, Mr. Yisroel Duchman, was a jolly and charming man who often encouraged his acquaintances to increase their Jewish observance. That year the organization was honoring Mr. Dennis Eckstein, a successful businessman in the air-conditioning field and Mr. Duchman's close friend.

Mr. Duchman enjoyed speaking to the Rebbe in Russian, a language that even the Rebbe's aides did not know. He once told the Rebbe, "I don't even want the mice to understand what I tell you," to which the Rebbe smiled.

At the meeting between the Shamir board members and the Rebbe, Duchman told the Rebbe, "I want you to know that Dennis [Eckstein] puts on *tefillin* every day. He is happy to fulfill this mitzvah, and does so openly and proudly."

The Rebbe, concerned that Mr. Duchman would announce this fact to the entire crowd at the dinner, responded, in Russian, that doing so might hurt Dennis' feelings. The Rebbe continued, "You cannot publicize this, because it will emphasize that until now he did not don tefillin. This is something you should not do."

Sharing

G-d gives out talent and
money as He sees fit.
It is our responsibility
to recognize that our
talents and assets should be
used to help those who have less.

" Redemption

Redeem yourself by
becoming a *hasid*.
Hasidim are kind
to themselves and to
others; they love their
fellows, G-d and
His Torah.

Just Like Yourself

While we may be aware of our personal flaws, for the most part we
cover them up well with self-love.
We need to do the same for others—
overlook their flaws. Especially since
we never truly know what's going on
inside another person's
mind and heart.

Be Honest

When a friend unknowingly errs
—due to ignorance or blindness—
you can either ignore what happened,
or honestly approach the situation
and try to explore the underlying issue.
Being condescending will not work;
speaking honestly from the heart will make
a difference. By ignoring the situation,
you are partially at fault for future
issues that may arise.
This will ultimately create
tension in your relationship and will
sit heavily on your conscience.

Decision Making

Only G-d makes decisions on His own. Conversely, we should always make an effort to consult with others. This is especially true when it comes to communal matters.

PATIENCE FOR THE NUDNIK

Rabbi Binyomin Klein served as the Rebbe's aide for three decades. Throughout that time he continually marveled at the Rebbe's immense patience, his approaching each person as if he or she were the only person in existence at that moment. The Rebbe's focus on each individual was steadfast.

Until the early 1980s, hundreds would arrive weekly for private audiences with the Rebbe. Later, thousands would meet with the Rebbe for a few brief moments on Sundays, where the Rebbe would give each visitor a dollar to give to charity. There were no criteria to meet with the Rebbe. The Rebbe seldom interrupted someone mid-sentence. At the summation of the meeting the Rebbe would only slightly indicate that their time had come to a close, and the visitor would understand the cue.

Once, a woman asked if she could speak with the Rebbe last, despite the fact that she'd scheduled an early appointment. When her turn finally arrived, the hour was very late. She spoke to the Rebbe for quite some time, with no indication of finishing. The Rebbe listened patiently. Rabbi Klein entered the room and told her that the audience was ending, yet she continued to speak.

When the conversation seemed to be completed, the Rebbe stood up and prepared to go home. However, the woman continued to speak, and the Rebbe listened as he put his coat on and headed to the doorway. The Rebbe wished her well and headed home.

Upon arriving home, the Rebbe phoned Rabbi Klein, who was still in the office, and said, "Please arrange for two students to escort the woman to her home in a taxi. I will pay for the taxi."

The Rebbe (left) during an audience in his study at Lubavitch world headquarters, 1960's..

Giving

Give a coin to a pauper,
although you do not owe
him or her anything.
G-d will reciprocate in kind
and grant you abundant blessings,
although He owes you nothing.

Middle Class Donations

Whether you donated a great amount or a small amount, according to your capability, G-d considers it as having a part in the entirety of the positive project. For without your effort, the entirety of the project would not be possible.

EMBARRASSING THE INMATES

In 1981, Rabbi Sholom Ber Lipskar and his wife, Chana, began to make weekly visits to local jails. These visits included learning sessions, holiday events and Jewish observance. Thus Rabbi Lipskar established the Aleph Institute in 1984.

The national organization catered to the spiritual and religious needs of inmates, including obtaining kosher food. One of the larger programs they developed was the establishment of religious furlough programs for prisoners, which would involve them in religious training and educational activities. The temporary freedom for these inmates, most of whom would be released within a year, was regarded as a way of easing them back into society.

The furlough program would take place at the Rabbinical College of America in Morristown, New Jersey. The inmates would spend two weeks delving into topics on Jewish learning, observance and inspiration. In 1985, a group of over a dozen inmates spent Shabbat in Brooklyn, New York.

During Shabbat afternoon the Rebbe presided over a hasidic gathering that included scholarly talks and the singing of intense melodies that created a unique camaraderie that uplifted all in attendance. Because it was Shabbat, there was no use of microphones. Many, wanting to catch every word, would remain in the synagogue in order to claim a good spot from which to listen to the Rebbe. Rabbi Lipskar reserved a table and asked a group of students to save the place for the visiting inmates. He also arranged for a translator who could sit beside the inmates and translate the Rebbe's words.

At the conclusion of the morning services the inmates left the synagogue for their afternoon meal, with plans to return shortly after, while Rabbi Lipskar remained. At the time the gathering typically began, all eyes were suddenly drawn to the staircase. The Rebbe's aide had come down alone. All were surprised, as the

Inmates on religious furlough listen to a lecture by Rabbi Sholom Ber Lipskar.

Rebbe rarely arrived late, and was always in the company of an aide. The aide sought out Rabbi Lipskar, who approached immediately. The aide had a message from the Rebbe regarding the prisoners.

The Rebbe had requested: "The prisoners should not sit together, so as not to attract attention, which may embarrass them. Rather, they should sit dispersed amongst the crowd, which will not highlight their status."

Superiority

The human being is not just
superior to G-d's earlier creations
of earth, vegetation and animals;
there is a wide chasm between
them. Humans have the capacity
to recognize the Creator, and this
recognition is the purpose
of creation.

PURPOSE

Punishment? 〝〟

G-d's precepts are not punishments. Rather, Jewish observance is an antidote to the daily grind and challenges of life. At times, we may see it as taxing and laborious to observe Torah and mitzvahs, but ultimately it is for our wellbeing.

" " The Defensive

When we find ourselves subject to outside influences in increasing intensity, we need to spiritually strengthen ourselves from a deep place within. We do this by expressing our resolve to maintain our Jewish heritage, tradition and observance.

Evolution

Through the history of the Jewish nation, our lifestyles have changed dramatically. We have changed our manner of clothing, language, location and more. However, throughout the upheavals, expulsions, atrocities and travels, one element did not change: Jewish observance.

NOTHING IS NEW

William Frankel, editor of the *Jewish Chronicle,* was staunchly anti-establishment, and gathered a team of like-minded journalists who traversed the globe to report the news and the global Jewish climate. He headed to the United States in the fall of 1960, expecting a cold reception; on his previous visit to America in the late 1940s, the British were despised by many local Jews for their unwanted involvement in the biblical Holy Land. He was surprised to be received so warmly this time around.

The editor headed to Brooklyn on Simchat Torah, one of the most joyous days of the Jewish calendar. He spent the day in three hasidic courts: Satmar, Bobov and Lubavitch. He was impressed by all of them. Of his visit to Lubavitch, he later wrote, "They sang and chanted in perfect unison and good humor, and, as the singing grew more intense, they stamped or clapped rhythmically."

A few days later he returned for an audience with the Rebbe. He spent one and a half hours with the Rebbe. Frankel later described the Rebbe, "His face is unlined, his eyes deep-set and bright; his rather full lips do not seem to move when he talks, perhaps to conserve strength for all those he must meet night after night... He listens hard and speaks quickly, not without any animation of the face or body, until he smiles—a beautifully gentle smile which transforms his features."

Mr. Frankel drilled the Rebbe about American issues, Israel affairs, Jewish dilemmas and British concerns. The Rebbe's answers came quickly. The editor was surprised, and questioned how the Rebbe had such swift responses.

The Rebbe said: "Why not? There are no new problems. In the long history of the Jewish people there have been all kinds of problems, and no matter what we have to face, we can find a parallel and the answer in our history."

The Rebbe in his study, surrounded by piles of Jewish scholarly texts, circa mid-1970s.

The Temple Within

Just as with the physical death of the
body, where the soul still survives—it
has only entered the spiritual world
of truth—so too, one can only destroy
the physical Holy Temple in Jerusalem,
built from wood, gold and silver; but
the spiritual temple within each and
every one of us, no one
can ever destroy.

Jewish Identity

"Estrangement" from one's Jewish heritage is an impossibility. For estrangement can apply only to an external entity; one cannot be estranged from himself! In this instance, Jewish heritage is part and parcel of every Jew's identity and part of his genes, by virtue of tens of generations of ancestors.

ANOTHER FORM OF CHARITY

In the late 1970s Yoel Freundlich, a London jeweler, brought his young son, Shimon, to New York to spend time with the Rebbe. The duo was given a 2:00 AM appointment to meet privately with the Rebbe. The father instructed his son to be on his best behavior during the audience.

The meeting, however, extended longer than planned. The young child began to look for toys in the room, but found none. He proceeded to open the window blinds, when the Rebbe called his name.

The Rebbe, holding a dollar in his hand, asked Shimon, "Do you know what this is?" The child responded that it was *tzedakah*. The Rebbe smiled and asked, "What is *tzedakah*?" to which Shimon responded, "Charity." The Rebbe smiled and asked, "What is charity?" The boy then said, "*Tzedakah*." The two toyed back and forth several times.

The Rebbe looked at Shimon and said, "There are two types of charity. There is charity with money, and there is charity one does with his physical body, to care and to share with somebody else. I want you to know that sometimes caring and sharing for someone else is more effective than giving money to charity."

A Chabad representative assists a college student to fulfill a Mitzvah during the holiday of Sukkot.

Who's First?

Before you can rule over the world, you need to rule over yourself, i.e., over your earthly nature and animalistic interests. This may be accomplished with diligent Torah study and intense effort. Once you have mastered yourself, you can influence the world.

Not Just You

When you do not fulfill
your mission in this world,
it is not just a personal
loss, but a global one.
The whole world
misses out.

NOT ONLY ABOUT YOU

Berel Futerfas and Avraham Shemtov, two students in their late teens, were travelling in 1953 from their homes in London, England, to Brooklyn, New York, to spend the Jewish holidays with the Rebbe.

They planned to embark on the *Queen Mary* ship just three days before Yom Kippur, which meant that they would still be aboard for the holy day.

They reported their travel plans to the Rebbe, and began their voyage. On the eve of Yom Kippur they received a telegram from the Rebbe via Royal Mail Ship (RMS), with a blessing to be inscribed and sealed for a good new year. The Rebbe added that the blessing should extend to other passengers aboard the ship, instructing the students to not only consider themselves, but others too.

The Rebbe wrote:

> And you should explain to those that are traveling with you, by divine individual providence—for everyone's benefit—to make an effort to return to G-d, regret any past transgressions and acceptance of the good in the future. And G-d should grant you all success. Menachem Schneerson.

The Queen Marry.

Never Enough

Our sages say: "One who has a hundred wants two hundred; one who has two hundred wants four hundred." Achievement whets the desire for even greater achievements, and at a faster pace. This is true regarding material wealth, and even more so it is necessary regarding spiritual achievements, in fulfilling G-d's will.

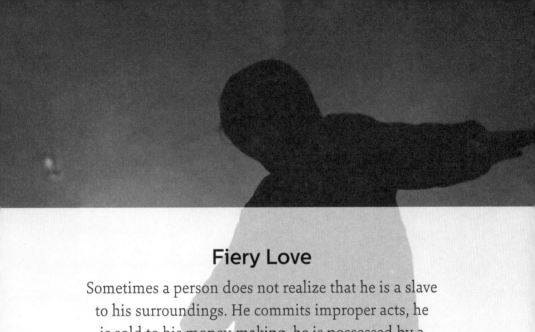

Fiery Love

Sometimes a person does not realize that he is a slave
to his surroundings. He commits improper acts, he
is sold to his money-making, he is possessed by a
desire for honor, and is a prisoner to his desires. By
awakening the fiery love of G-d imbued in your soul,
you free yourself from this enslavement.

IT IS NOT ALL ABOUT MONEY

Mr. Berel Weiss, a Hungarian Holocaust survivor, was living in a Displaced Persons camp in Germany following the Holocaust, unsure how to rebuild or reclaim his life. He saw a notice in a bulletin that mentioned the sixth Chabad rebbe, the Rebbe Rayatz, and decided to move to the United States to be nearer to him.

However, Mr. Weiss and the Rebbe never had the opportunity to meet. Instead Mr. Weiss moved to Los Angeles, where he encountered Rabbi Shmuel Dovid Raichik, the legendary Chabad-Lubavitch emissary to the West Coast.

Mr. Weiss was climbing the business ladder when he accompanied Rabbi Raichik to meet the Rebbe in 1961. The young businessman was very moved, and approached the Rebbe while the congregants sang. Mr. Weiss told the Rebbe that he would pledge $100,000 to Chabad activities.

The next day, during a private audience, the Rebbe asked, "And what will you give me?"

The philanthropist, considering his recent pledge, again affirmed, "Whatever amount of money the Rebbe asks for, I will give!"

The Rebbe responded, "The next time you come for an appointment, bring 10,000 pages of the Talmud that you learned!"

Trust

Don't place your trust
in flesh and blood,
even the greatest sage.
Trust only in G-d,
the source of
all blessing.

Revolutions

Our mission in this world is not about engaging in heavenly endeavors and revolutions that are detached from daily life. Rather, our mission is to create a dwelling place for G-d here in this world, in a peaceful way, through actions and daily Jewish observance that engage the physical reality. If there is a need for a revolution, it will happen through divine intervention.

A Small World

You are a small world. You have tendencies that are earthly and animalistic, and a yearning for the divine that is unique to man. In your sleep you are almost lifeless, like the earth. When you eat, you are no different than an animal. But when you use your intellectual and spiritual capacities to recognize G-d, then you have fulfilled the purpose of your creation, for you were born to use your unique human faculties to do what is good and right.

Creation's Purpose

We do not celebrate the creation of the world on the first day of its creation; we celebrate on Rosh Hashanah, the day of man's creation. For the ultimate purpose of the heavens, the earth and all worldly creations is the human being.

 ## The Soul's Descent

Your soul has no interest in physical pleasure; it wants nothing but to live in the spiritual realms. But G-d sent it down to this material world and clothed it in a physical body. For decades your soul lives in this world—against its will—only to fulfill G-d's desire. Yet the holiness it creates by carrying out G-d's will is infinite, and certainly worth the spiritual pain of the descent.

Creating Miracles

This world is not separate from the higher worlds,
but is part of a continuum.

Everything in this world is influenced by the worlds
above it.

Similarly, a miracle stems from beyond our world,
and is brought down from above when one
connects with G-d through prayer, Torah and Jewish
observance. These acts affect this world and the
ones above it in ways that are beyond calculation.

Furthermore, the ability to create such wide
influence is present within each person.

ESSAYS ON LIFE

By Rabbi Yitzchak Menachem Weinberg
The Rabbi of Tolna

Do You Feel Another's Pain?

When we hear that something horrible has befallen another individual, G-d forbid, do we feel their pain? Or do we simply move on with life?

What is the first thing we do when we hear about a fatal accident, for example?

Most of us wonder: Where was it—near my house or my child's school? Could the victim have been a family member or a friend?

When we hear that it was nowhere near anyone we know, we breathe a sigh of relief and continue with our day. Sure, we are saddened, but if our family and children are fine, life continues...

Rabbi Pinchas Menachem Alter, the late leader of the Gur hasidic dynasty (d. 1996), told me a story that happened in 1949.

One of the disciples of Rabbi Yisrael Alter of Gur, known as the "Beis Yisroel," was very wealthy, and at one point lived in New Zealand due to his business dealings.

Once, on a trip to New York to visit his daughter, he entered an elevator only to be greeted by a Jew who asked where he hailed from. He responded that he had just arrived from New Zealand.

The stranger asked him, "Is there a *mikvah* (ritual bath) in New Zealand?" The wealthy man responded, "I am there for business, not a *mikvah*."

The stranger responded, "If a Jew finds himself somewhere, he must have a positive impact."

The elevator doors opened, and both men exited and went their separate ways.

The wealthy man asked his daughter, who was waiting for him nearby, regarding the identity of the man who rode in the elevator with him. She responded that he was Rabbi Menachem Mendel Schneerson, the son-in-law of the sixth Chabad Rebbe, who would later himself

become the seventh Rebbe.

Over forty years passed, during which time the businessman had aged significantly. He had long since left New Zealand and he was, again, visiting his daughter in New York. He decided to go to the Rebbe's Sunday dollar distribution.

When he greeted the Rebbe, the Rebbe asked, "Is there a *mikvah* already in New Zealand?"

The elderly man was clearly amazed.

"I asked him," Rabbi Alter continued, "'Tell me, what you were amazed by?'"

He responded that he was amazed by the Rebbe's memory; after all, forty years had elapsed since their elevator rendezvous!

"And I told him," Rabbi Alter concluded, "that what astounds me is what was on the Rebbe's mind for forty years—a *mikvah* in faraway New Zealand. And how bothered he was that there was none there…"

"Make here the Land of Israel," several Chabad rebbes stated.

What is the meaning of this statement? How can one take the Land of Israel—its holiness and unique qualities—and mimic that atmosphere in the Diaspora?

To explain, we turn to a discussion on Jewish law. On Shabbat we refrain, by biblical injunction, from carrying in a public domain. The rabbis further applied this restriction to an area not covered under this biblical law, for it is not a "public domain": an enclosed courtyard or neighborhood that contains multiple private dwellings. One may not carry between two private properties within this enclosure unless there is an *eruv* that "merges" the private properties.

The *eruv* consists of a food substance, usually bread or *matzah*, placed in one of the homes within the enclosure—but jointly owned by all those who live within the *eruv* parameters, so they could all technically come and eat of that bread.

In this regard, there is seemingly a contradiction between the Jerusalem Talmud and the Babylonian Talmud. The Jerusalem Talmud says that one needs only to designate the food as the *eruv*; however, one does not need to actually make a formal act of transaction to place the food into the ownership of the public (i.e., all who live within the enclosure). The Babylonian Talmud says that one would need to make such an act of transaction in order for the *eruv* to be effective.

The Rebbe explains that, in essence, there is no disagreement. For the Jerusalem Talmud, authored by sages living in the Land of Israel, is referring to an *eruv* created in that land; the Babylonian Talmud is referring to one outside of Israel.

The uniqueness of Israel is that it is natural for Jews to live there, and citizens feel an inborn attachment to each other. Outside of Israel, however, people are more preoccupied with their own lives, and feel less attached to their coreligionists.

The natural connection between Jews in Israel is reason why a transaction is not necessary for the *eruv* to take effect. However, outside of Israel, in order for unity, the merging of people's properties, to occur, one would need an actual transaction.

From this explanation, we might also understand the statement, "Make here the Land of Israel." This is a call for us to create in the Diaspora a unified atmosphere, a sense of belonging, which exists naturally only in the Land of Israel.

When the Rebbe would announce a new campaign, he would say, "When you meet someone on the street, share it with him." This is the essence of the Rebbe's message: what you know, share with others. We are all connected, and it's in our power to positively influence the people we encounter.

When you hear of a tragedy, try to generate compassion, and assist your fellow as much as you can.

When you know that someone near you is lacking in Jewish knowledge, try to reach out to him or her.

For, in essence, we are all one, like two hands on a single body.

Are You Successful?

We all seek quick success. We pursue individuals whom we deem "successful." Likewise, we run from our failures and are embarrassed to admit them.

The ever-present question is, "How can we be successful?"

Joseph is the first person referred to in the Torah as a "successful man." But at what venture in his life does this happen? When he was the beloved son in his father's home or when he was a viceroy in Egypt?

The answer, surprisingly, is neither. Joseph is referred to as a successful man when he was a slave to Potiphar, and then again when he was in the dark, dingy pit of an Egyptian prison.

Was this Joseph's success in life—to be sold by his brothers as a slave, only to be thrown into jail by the master he served faithfully?

The "Falsified" Contract

The Talmud tells us that there are several ways to validate the authenticity of a signed contract, to establish that it isn't a forgery. One method is to compare the signatures on the contract to a previous document with the same signatories. However, this document used to authenticate the current contested contract must have been verified by a court of law after its authenticity, too, was contested. Such a contract is considered weightier than another contract (even if its authenticity was also vouched for by a court) that was never the subject of any contention.

The Rebbe explains that a contract the people pronounce a forgery is like an individual who goes through a crisis, a letdown, a depressing fiasco. When the person overcomes the crisis, he is stronger; he can be a "contract" used to approve other "contracts." Essentially, without that bump in the road, he would not be as strong as he has become.

As such, the Rebbe offered a different definition

of success.

Success is not about an individual who has no flaws, who lives a perfect life. Joseph's life in jail was far from ideal; in fact, his spirit was broken. Success is when one goes through a crisis and, instead of falling prey to despair, stands up and declares that he or she will not be defeated.

When one burrows himself inside a hole, he has done the exact opposite. But when one utilizes that moment of despair, he comes out a stronger person, stronger than one who never experienced that challenge. That individual has developed the capacity to be stronger in yet more complex situations, for he has already overcome them.

Crying for "Naught"

How many times did the Rebbe cry of the danger that would befall Israel if the Sinai Desert is returned to Egypt?

The Rebbe corresponded with members of the Israeli government and military over the course of years about the grave situation that would be created by leaving Sinai. He developed close connections with these individuals, and they would often seek his counsel.

But the fact is that Sinai was ultimately returned to the Egyptians.

For an individual like the Rebbe to spend much of two years speaking about the safety of Jews in Israel only to be betrayed by the very people to whom he devoted so much energy, is what we would call the ultimate failure.

And had he felt like a failure, perhaps he would have written off the Israeli government saying, "You guys want to take your path, go ahead, but keep me out of it. You are not welcome in my office anymore."

However, two days after Sinai was evacuated, an Israeli general came to the Rebbe for a private audience. He had prepared many different reasons for why the Israeli government did not listen to the Rebbe's advice.

The Israeli general told me in these words, "What happened did not interest [the Rebbe] one iota; he had already turned the page. The Israel-Egypt border was now a new situation, and he wanted to know how it was being protected. He was worried about the security of those living in Israel."

Anyone could have asked the Rebbe: "The Israelis did not listen; they turned their backs on you. The situation flopped. Perhaps it's time to cut the ties?"

While we may think that the bottom line is success or failure, according to the Rebbe, success is measured differently. From Joseph, known as "the successful man" while imprisoned in Egypt, we learn that effort, and all that results from effort, is the real success. For Joseph, this meant that though he was imprisoned, he still employed tremendous effort to maintain the spiritual standards of his father's home.

One day, one of the Rebbe's aides encountered a certain individual in Lubavitch world headquarters. The aide asked this person, who lived in a certain New Jersey city: "Do you know this-and-this individual from your city?" When he responded affirmatively, the aide requested that he tell that person that the Rebbe's secretariat takes interest in how he is doing.

This individual in whom the aide expressed interest later related this story to me. When he received the message from the Rebbe's aide, he told the messenger that he had no strength to travel to Brooklyn to find out what this was all about, but he asked for the secretariat's phone number.

When he called, the aide told him as follows: "The Rebbe heard that there is a Jewish day school in your area that is on the brink of closure due to low student registration. Since you are the administrator of another school in the area, the Rebbe requested that you work on increasing the enrollment in that endangered school."

"But it's not of the same religious orientation as mine," he protested. "I do not feel that it is befitting for me to be involved with that school."

The aide responded that if he so wishes he could make an appointment for an audience with the Rebbe, at which point he could explain directly to the Rebbe why he feels that he shouldn't get involved. "However, you should know that the Rebbe feels that you are the best person for the job…"

Not wishing to disregard the Rebbe's wishes, he made an appointment. He prepared a long letter that contained eighteen reasons why he felt that he cannot take the position.

He handed the letter to the Rebbe. The Rebbe read it and asked him: "Tell me, are these eighteen explanations sufficient reason that eighteen—or more—children enrolled in the school should now lose the opportunity to have a Jewish education?

"If you accept the position, I am certain that G-d will broaden your resources—giving you more time and capabilities."

Leaving the Rebbe's office, he felt like a person on a mission. He threw himself into the task of increasing the school's enrollment. His efforts paid off, and enrollment tripled in a short time.

He wrote a very proud letter to the Rebbe, listing all his successes.

The Rebbe responded. Between his blessings and remarks, he also added in one word: "Success?"

The principal was stunned! A short while later found him once again in the Rebbe's room for a private audience.

"What was the comment on his letter supposed to mean?" he asked the Rebbe.

The Rebbe gently asked him to define success and then asked him whether one can herald as a success having a few dozen children enrolled in a school—when there are so many more children who still are receiving no Jewish education.

"But I tripled the enrollment," the individual protested. "Is that not considered success?"

The Rebbe explained to him that success means exerting effort; it's the continued struggle to do what is right.

That person walked out of the office with a new perspective on success. He understood that the Rebbe very much appreciated his efforts—but didn't want him to rest on his laurels; there was so much more to be done.

Success is a continual struggle in life.

I remind myself that prosperity is not always success, and crisis does not mean failure.

Success is measured by our struggles and efforts to do what is right. Success is not measured by forecasts, polls and the situations we find ourselves in. Success is when we turn struggle into empowerment, and then that very struggle will lead to other successes, each more powerful than the previous one.

Finding the Individuals
Within the Community

The biblical story relates that Korah was furious that his cousin Aaron was appointed as high priest and the sole progenitor of all future priests.

Moses explained that Aaron's appointment was not his own, but G-d's. Yet Korah continued to argue, and incited the Jewish nation to join him in revolt.

Moses informed Korah that on the following day Korah, his followers, and Aaron too would all offer incense to G-d. On that occasion, Moses assured, G-d would clearly identify the one He has chosen to be the leader. And at that point, the Torah tells us, Moses prayed to G-d, asking Him not to accept Korah's offering.

Rabbi Shlomo Yitzchaki, the famed biblical commentator Rashi, asks: Why did Moses need to pray? Was he not just acting on G-d's orders? Was it not G-d who appointed Aaron to his position? Would not G-d have to stand up, as it were, for His chosen one—even without Moses' supplication?

Rashi answers that Moses was not referring to the incense that would be offered in the next day's showdown. Rather, Moses knew that Korah and the rest of the mutineers had a part in the daily communal offerings brought in the Tabernacle on behalf of the entire nation; his prayer was that these offerings, too, should not be accepted by G-d.

Rabbi Chaim Joseph David Azulai, known as the Chida, explains that when speaking of a community, we are referring to two dynamics: a) A unified congregation, which joins a variety of people into one communal entity. b) The many individuals who make up the community.

The same holds true with communal offerings. On one hand, the entirety of the offering is

being offered by the singular unit known as the "community." On the other hand, every individual has a unique part in the offering.

And Moses prayed to G-d – not that the offering as a whole be rejected, but that the unique portions of incense that represented the members of the rebellious faction not be accepted.

A Letter for All

In the early 1980s the Rebbe, of righteous memory, began a campaign to encourage every Jew to buy a letter in a Torah scroll. The campaign was based on the biblical commandment that every individual write or acquire their very own Torah scroll.

The Rebbe then asked (in the course of a hasidic gathering on December 15th, 1981): Why is it that, for many centuries, the majority of Jews did not own their own Torahs?

And he justified the prevailing custom by offering an explanation similar to the Chida's: When a person is called up for an *aliyah* at a Torah reading, it is as if the scribe wrote the entire Torah for that individual. How so? Because, though that individual is part of the community, he is entirely unique. And when he is called up to the Torah, it is that uniqueness that is revealed, his individual part in the Torah. That, the Rebbe explains, is how he fulfills the commandment of writing a Torah scroll.

Many Individuals, Many Tasks

There is a Chabad saying, used pejoratively, "It did not affect, it did not impact." This means that Torah knowledge should not just be a scholarly, theoretical and conceptual discussion, but rather, should have an effect on the individual.

The Rebbe led the worldwide Chabad-Lubavitch community, but he was also a leader of world Jewry. The Rebbe felt connected to every single Jew. He turned to individuals with no background in Jewish practice and encouraged them to put on tefillin, to light Shabbat candles. He taught that every action, even a "small" good deed, is precious.

The Rebbe often expressed the great pleasure G-d experiences from even one good deed, done by a single Jew, even once in his or her life.

This is the way he brought tens of thousands of Jews to do hundreds of thousands of mitzvahs.

One might have imagined that the Rebbe's standards for his own followers, and his expectations of them, might have declined, since his outreach extended to people entirely unaffiliated with Judaism. However, the Rebbe continued to encourage already practicing Jews to advance in their Jewish observance and learning. We can see this clearly from two letters on the same subject, written on the very same day, to two different individuals.

The Chabad custom is that on the wedding day, the groom publicly reviews a hasidic discourse about marriage. In the first letter, the Rebbe responded to a groom who told the Rebbe that he had said only one paragraph at his wedding.

"Why would you say only a portion of the discourse? Are you not aware of the great significance of this discourse, which includes teachings from every one of the Chabad Rebbes? What was done cannot be undone; however, gather a group of ten as soon as you receive this letter, and say the entire discourse."

In another letter, the Rebbe responded to a Chabad emissary who wrote about a frequent visitor and student at the Chabad House who was planning his wedding. The Rebbe wrote that the emissary should encourage the groom to say at the wedding at least a few lines from the discourse…

Both letters written on the same day, by the same Rebbe. However, the Rebbe addressed each person based on their varying situations. Each groom's individual abilities needed to be uniquely utilized.

Understanding People

A professor once wrote to the Rebbe, trying to understand how G-d could have let the Holocaust happen. As always, the Rebbe responded brilliantly. However, I was most touched by what the Rebbe wrote towards the end of the letter (adapted here): "I noticed that you signed now using your secular name. I recall that ten years ago I received an invitation to your son's wedding, and there you signed with your Jewish name…"

Yes, it is amazing that the Rebbe remembered.

Ten years had passed since the wedding—a wedding he did not attend—and this was only one among tens of thousands of wedding invitations that he received over those years. However, the fact that this letter attests to the Rebbe's phenomenal memory is not what, in my opinion, makes this letter remarkable.

The Rebbe continues in his letter: "You write that you cannot believe in G-d after what happened during the Holocaust. Your letter demonstrates the great hatred you harbor towards the Germans for their barbaric acts... As a daughter of the Jewish nation, I now ask you: why do you use your secular name that's sourced in the German language?"

And he concludes, "Perhaps you will do me a favor, and from today on, start using your Jewish name."

It is understandable that the Rebbe responded to her question about the Holocaust. However, in his great love for every individual, he did not satisfy himself with doing just that. The Rebbe considered what Jewish act the professor could incorporate into her life—an act that she herself would want to do, for in her mind it would equate to doing something that would make a personal stand against the barbaric Nazis.

This is the way the Rebbe saw things. For every individual, there is their unique way of encouraging them in their Jewish growth.

To the Chabad disciple, the Rebbe would instruct regarding which hasidic discourses to study, or the extra stringency in Jewish law that he should adopt. From the Israeli soldier, the Rebbe would request that he put on tefillin every day. And the businesswoman, the Rebbe would invite to light Shabbat and holiday candles.

There are so many different people in the world, with their own understanding and with their own way of acting. The Rebbe guided each and every one of them to grow in their unique way.

And to the Rebbe, even that one small act was an entire world.

Glossary

Aliyah. An ascent. In a prayer service, the term describes the honor of being called to make a blessing on the Torah scroll before it is read.

Chabad. An acronym for the Hebrew words *chochma*, *binah* and *daat*—"wisdom, understanding and knowledge." Chabad is a branch of the Hasidic movement (see below) that takes an intellectual approach to the service of G-d. Chabad is also known for bolstering Jewish life across the globe.

G-d. To indicate its holiness, the divine name is not written in its entirety, even in translation.

Hassidism; Hasid; Hasidic. From the Hebrew word *hesed*, "kindness," the Hasidic movement was founded in the 18th century by Rabbi Israel the son of Eliezer, later known as the Baal Shem Tov. Hasidic philosophy uses the mystical teachings of the Kabbalah to illuminate the deeper significance of Jewish prayer and ritual. The Hasid serves G-d with love and joy, recognizing the role of divine providence in every aspect of his or her life.

Lubavitch; Lubavitcher. Lit. "the town of love," Lubavitch is the Yiddish name for the Russian village where the Chabad movement was based for over a century. The movement, its followers and leaders became known as "Lubavitch" or "Lubavitchers."

Mikvah. Lit. "a gathering of water." A *mikvah* is a ritual bath or a pool of water, of prescribed source and volume. Immersion in a *mikvah* bestows spiritual purity.

Mitzvah. Lit. "a commandment." Referring to Jewish observance, but the word is also used loosely for any good deed.

Rebbe. Lit. "teacher," the term also refers to a Hasidic leader. In this book, "the Rebbe" is the seventh Lubavitcher Rebbe, Rabbi Menachem Mendel Schneerson (1902–1994).

Rebbetzin. The honorary title for the wife of a rabbi. In this book it refers to Rebbetzin Chaya Mushka Schneerson (1901–1988), the wife of the Rebbe (see above).

Shabbat. Day of rest. The Jewish Sabbath commemorates the completion of the six days of creation and G-d's resting on the seventh day. It is observed each week from sunset on Friday until Saturday night with festive meals and special prayer services.

Simchat Torah. Lit. "rejoicing with the Torah," the holiday that celebrates the completion of the yearly Torah-reading cycle. Simchat Torah is observed on the second day of the festival of Shemini Atzeret, which follows Sukkot (see below).

Sukkah; **Sukkot**. Sukkot is the eight-day festival which follows the high holy days of Rosh Hashanah and Yom Kippur. The *sukkah*, a small hut erected outdoors, commemorates the clouds that protected the Jews as they traveled through the desert from Egypt to the land of Israel. During the holiday, all meals and regular activities are conducted in the *sukkah*.

Tefillin. Black leather boxes containing parchment scrolls worn by men on the arm and the head during weekday morning prayers in fulfillment of the command, "You shall bind them as a sign upon your hand, and they shall be for you a reminder between your eyes" (Deuteronomy 6:8).

Torah. The Bible (Five Books of Moses); teaching; the Torah scroll; used loosely for the general corpus of Jewish teachings.

Sources & Credits

Adapted freely from the correspondence and conversations of the
Lubavitcher Rebbe. Below are the dates and sources
(note that several of the quotes are not published and
are therefore not sourced to any specific volume):

• •

Page 12 **Success** December 4, 1974 (Igrot Kodesh [IK], vol. 30, p. 54). ¶ p. 13 **Bliss?** August 29, 1956. ¶ p. 14 **Keeping Occupied** 1947 (IK, vol. 29, p. 282). ¶ p. 15 **Purpose** January 9, 1974 (IK, vol. 28, p. 67). ¶ p. 16 **Choice** fall 1955 (Igrot Melech [IM], p. 18). ¶ p. 18 **Return** fall 1960 and fall 1967 (ibid, pages 34 and 58). ¶ p. 19 **Evil's Limits** fall 1966 (ibid, p. 20). ¶ p. 20 **The Atom in You** fall 1955 (ibid, p. 19). ¶ p. 22 **G-d's Love** fall 1960 (ibid, p. 35). ¶ p. 22 **G-d's Envoy** fall 1974 (ibid, p. 130). ¶ p. 24 **The Power of One** fall 1964 (ibid, p. 49). ¶ p. 25 **Many Creatures, One Human** fall 1964 (ibid, p. 48). ¶ p. 28 **Self-Respect** September 17, 1973 (ibid, pp. 339ff). ¶ p. 29 **Your Virtues** November 27, 1972 (ibid p. 54). ¶ p. 30 **The Effort** December 23, 1974 (IK, vol. 30, p. 79). ¶ p. 31 **Moving On** August 29, 1956. ¶ p. 32 **Speech** 1974 (IK, vol. 29, p. 273). ¶ p. 33 **Thoughts** April 17, 1974 (ibid, p. 140). ¶ p. 34 **The Flame** December 8, 1974 (IK, vol. 30, p. 62). ¶ p. 36 **Your Capabilities** February 18, 1975 (ibid p.

125). ¶ p. 37 **Uplifting** December 6, 1974 (ibid p. 57). ¶ p. 40 **Spiritual Heights** December 10, 1973 (IM p. 117). ¶ p. 41 **Quantity or Quality** fall 1969 (IM p. 68). ¶ p. 44 **The Doctor** May 20, 1975 and November 8, 1973 (ibid p. 221 and IK vol. 29, p. 23). ¶ p. 48 **Dieting** May 22, 1973, April 26, 1979 and letter from 1979 (IK, vol. 28, p. 210). ¶ p. 52 **Depressing Dreams** Undated (Leshema Ozen [1991 edition], p. 341). ¶ p. 56 **The Natural Order** March 14, 1974 (IK, vol. 29, p. 113). ¶ p. 57 **Smoking** October 24, 1976; **Regret** November 22, 1973 (IK vol. 29, p. 30). ¶ p. 64 **Disappointment** May 1973 (IK vol. 28, p. 219). ¶ p. 65 **Business Focus** October 28, 1972 (ibid, p. 25). ¶ p. 66 **Negative Business** February 20, 1973 (ibid, p. 133). ¶ p. 67 **Constant Worry** August 31, 1973 (ibid, p. 309). ¶ p. 68 **A New Occupation** 1974 (ibid, p. 267). ¶ p. 69 **Mother on the Job** October 1973 (ibid, p. 12). ¶ p. 70 **Livelihood Attitude** September 21, 1962. ¶ p. 74 **Protection** November 7, 1972 (IK vol. 28, p. 39). ¶ p. 75 **Permanent** 1974 (IK vol. 29, p. 281). ¶ p. 76 **Smile Back** November 1, 1972 (IK vol. 28, p. 30). ¶ p. 77 **Change** October 12, 1972 (ibid, p. 21). ¶ p. 82 **The Middle** 1975 (IK vol. 30, p. 302). ¶ p. 83 **The Goal** January 13, 1975 (ibid, p. 91). ¶ p. 88 **Sharing** December 11, 1972 (IM, p. 94). ¶ p. 89 **Redemption** November 17, 1953 (ibid, p. 11). ¶ p. 90 **Just Like Yourself** October 7, 1976 (ibid, p. 161). ¶ p. 92 **Be Honest** January 8, 1973 (IK, vol. 28, p. 99ff). ¶ p. 93 **Decision Making** October 28, 1974 (IK, vol. 30, p. 15). ¶ p. 96 **Giving** October 1973 (IK, vol. 29, p. 11). ¶ p. 97 **Middle Class Donations** March 14, 1974 (ibid, p. 112). ¶ p. 100

Superiority fall 1955 (IM, p. 18). ¶ p. 104 **Punishment?** January 8, 1973 (IK, vol. 28, p. 99) ¶ p. 105 **The Defensive** November 5, 1974 (IK vol. 30, p. 19). ¶ p. 106 **Evolution** March 24, 1975 (ibid, p. 176). ¶ p. 110 **The Temple Within** winter 1974 (IK, vol. 29, p. 76). ¶ p. 111 **Jewish Identity** November 20, 1973 (ibid, p. 28). ¶ p. 114 **Who's First?** September 28, 1959 (IM, p. 31). ¶ p. 115 **Not Just You** September 28, 1959 (ibid, p. 32). ¶ p. 118 **Never Enough** spring 1974 (ibid, p. 165). ¶ p. 119 **Fiery Love** April 3, 1974 (ibid, p. 128). ¶ p. 122 **Trust** November 22, 1973 (ibid, p. 30). ¶ p. 123 **Revolutions** 1967 (Heichal Menachem, vol. 2, p. 90). ¶ p. 124 **A Small World** August 30, 1953 (IM, p. 9). ¶ p. 126 **Creation's Purpose** August 30, 1953 (ibid, p. 8). ¶ p. 126 **The Soul's Descent** November 17, 1953 (ibid, p. 11). ¶ p. 128 **Creating Miracles** Interview, March 7, 1960.

Photos:

Marc Asnin, Michel Setboun, Joe Chahwan, Aleph Institute, Tyagan Miller, Grayson Dantzic, Yosef Lewis, NCFJE, Algemeiner Journal and Michele Studios/The Kahan family.

Some images were not marked with the photographer's name.

We regret any omissions.

Acknowledgements

Creating this booklet, from collecting material to researching stories and anecdotes, would not have been possible without the assistance of many. With special thanks to:

My wife, Chana Raizel, for her constant encouragement, input and constructive criticism.

Chana Lewis-Silberg, who tirelessly reviewed, commented and clarified the material. Elana Rudnick and her dedicated team at Design Is Yummy for the fantastic design work.

I offer my thanks to those who reviewed the collection in its entirety: Alex Heppenheimer, Rabbi Avraham Kievman, Rabbi Aaron Leib Raskin, Chana Sharfstein and Rabbi Moshe Zaklikofsky. To all those who shared their personal stories that are in this booklet.

To the late Rabbi Simcha Zirkind, of blessed memory, whose encouragement and infectious drive for excellence is the motivation behind these publications.

My gratitude to Marc Asnin for always being eager and ready to assist in every way. With thanks to Michel Setboun and Joe Chahwan for granting me permission to use their wonderful photos.

Thank you to Moshe N. Barouk, Pesach Burston, Yitzchok Frankfurter, Shimon Freundlich, Chaim Baruch Halberstam, Mayer Harlig, Yitzchok Yehudah Holtzman, Avraham Jaffe, Moshe Gombo, The Kahn Family, Mendy Katz, Rabbi Shalom Ber Lipskar, Jakub Redziniak, Ezzi Shaffran, Shimmy Shaffran, Zalman Sosover, Marc Wilson, Menachem Wolff and Hindy Zirkind, for sharing your stories, information and photos from your collections.

The first printing of this book was dedicated to Shira and Yossi Avtzon, Mottel and Rochel Bronstein, and Ruchie Stillman, the amazing people who influenced me deeply in my youth. Their selfless example still guides me in my daily life.

This current volume is dedicated to Lorne Rozovsky, who showed me how to make complex subjects understandable to people who don't have a background in Jewish studies. From our first meeting in 2006 until his passing in 2013, we became good friends. I miss him sorely.

I offer unique thanks to the Almighty for granting me the strength and courage to continue with this project.

Dovid Zaklikowski

In loving memory of
Mottel Sharfstein

With the courage of a soldier, Mottel continued life under the most difficult circumstances. First there was a walker, then a wheelchair. Eventually he required assistance with all his daily living activities. His steady, strong hands, the trademark of his trade, could no longer turn the pages of his beloved scholarly books. Yet despite this gradual and inexorable loss of independence, he persevered and lived life to the fullest.

With great difficulty he climbed the steep stairs to the synagogue to pray each day and attend Torah classes. He participated in local events, lectures and joyous occasions. He even visited neighbors who needed comfort. His eyes would sparkle with joy as he held out his arms to hug his grandchildren.

He endured the challenges with quiet dignity, grace and hope. The phrase "thank G-d" was always on his lips.

Mottel provided us with a powerful example of a life of faith, honesty and humility. Filled with love for family and all people, dedicated to Torah and mitzvahs, he embraced life and made every moment count.

לע"נ הרב **מרדכי אליעזר** בן **אברהם זאב** ע"ה **שארפשטיין**

More in the series:

Advice for Life: Education

Advice for Life: Marriage

Advice for Life: From Life to Life

Dignified Differences: A Special Soul

Learning on the Job: Jewish Career Lessons

Hasidic Archives books are available in special discounts for bulk purchases in the United States for corporations, institutions, and other organizations. For more information, please contact us at RebbeAdvice@Gmail.com.